Pg. 154

STEAM JOBS FOR GAMERS

BY SAM RHODES

CAPSTONE PRESS
a capstone imprint

Edge Books are published by Capstone Press,
1710 Roe Crest Drive
North Mankato, Minnesota 56003
www.mycapstone.com

Library of Congress Cataloging-in-Publication Data
Names: Rhodes, Sam (Samuel David), 1983- author.
Title: STEAM jobs for gamers / by Sam Rhodes.
Description: North Mankato, Minnesota : Capstone Press, [2019] |
   Series: Edge books. Steam jobs | Includes bibliographical references and index. |
   Audience: Ages 8-14.
Identifiers: LCCN 2018011852 (print) | LCCN 2018014354 (ebook) |
   ISBN 9781543531015 (eBook PDF) | ISBN 9781543530933 (hardcover) |
   ISBN 9781543530971 (pbk.)
Subjects: LCSH: Computer games—Programming—Vocational guidance—Juvenile literature. | Video
   games—Design—Vocational guidance—Juvenile literature.
Classification: LCC QA76.76.C672 (ebook) | LCC QA76.76.C672 R536 2019 (print) |
   DDC 794.8/1023—dc23
LC record available at https://lccn.loc.gov/2018011852

Editorial Credits

Editor: Lauren Dupuis-Perez
Book Designer: Sara Radka
Production Specialist: Kathy McColley

Image Credits

Getty Images: adventtr, cover (back), AF-studio, background, Avalon_Studio, 15 (right), Charley Gallay, 23, Handout, 7, Justin Sullivan, 20, Kerkez, cover, mattjeacock, 12, PeopleImages, 10, Studio Fernanda Calfat, 27 (top), Veronika Surovtseva, 15 (left), vgajic, 11; Newscom: xavier de torres/ MAXPPP, 28, Xinhua/Liang Sen, 21, ZUMA Press/Ringo Chiu, 18; Shutterstock: alphaspirit, 22, antb, 24, design36, 16, ESB Professional, 8, frantic00, 27 (bottom), Gorodenkoff, 4, 6, julia_belutskaya, 25, KOKTARO, 9, Marcin Roszkowski 17 (top), nd3000, 29, pixelparticle, 1, Rawpixel.com, 19, REDPIXEL.PL, 13, valeriiaarnaud, 26, Vandrage Artist, 14, vectorfusionart, 17 (bottom)

Printed and bound in the USA.
PA017

TABLE OF CONTENTS

LEVELING UP

Gamers all over the world compete in video game competitions for cash prizes.

What was it like to fly a bomber in World War II (1939–1945)? Can you imagine fighting crowds of zombies or riding a dinosaur? It may not be possible to do these things in real life, but video games can give you a glimpse into experiences like these and more.

Video games are not just fun pastimes, though. They can also lead gamers to exciting careers in many **STEAM** fields. Some gamers might find they have a passion for the audio and visual aspects of games. Others might want to explore the computer science behind video games. Still other gamers might focus on the overall experience of a video game. From creating virtual reality (VR) worlds to script writing, gamers with a STEAM education are leveling up!

STEAM—the abbreviation for science, technology, engineering, art, and mathematics

CHAPTER 1
VIDEO GAME DESIGNERS

BY DESIGN

The first game was a massive hit. Now the pressure is on. The sequel has to be even better. It needs faster vehicles, more challenging puzzles, cleaner graphics, and another unique story. These important elements come down to the leadership of one person: the game designer. The game designer settles in front of her computer, and she gets to work.

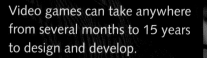

Video games can take anywhere from several months to 15 years to design and develop.

The first step of making a video game is coming up with the overall design. The designer creates a **concept** for the game and builds a blueprint. The blueprint is called a game design document (GDD). The GDD shows themes, style, characters, missions, and story lines for the game. What objects are available to the character? What puzzles must they solve? What will make this game fun and challenging? The game designer must answer these questions.

After finishing the GDD, the designer shows it to the studio managers. If they like the GDD and the concept for the game, the game moves into production.

EDUCATION

Game designers should have a strong background in the following STEAM subjects:

- **computer science**
- **animation**
- **creative writing**
- **software engineering**

STEAM FACT

Game designer Shigeru Miyamoto created Mario Brothers in 1983. Mario Brothers became the most successful video game series ever. Fans have bought more than 577 million games.

concept—an idea for a new way to build or create something

Video games bring in $105 billion worldwide every year.

IN PRODUCTION

During production the game designer works with the rest of the development team. The team includes writers, artists, and programmers. Throughout the process, the designer reviews the game. Sometimes the team encounters problems. Limits to technology or budget may creep in. The designer works with the team on solutions. The designer then adjusts the GDD to reflect the new plan.

Once the team has built all the different pieces, the designer oversees game testing. The designer needs to make sure that the game is easy to use and that the game controls feel comfortable. The designer then tests the different levels to make sure that they challenge players but are not completely impossible.

GAMES ON THE GO

Some designers choose to work on mobile games. While **console** games take years to develop, mobile games usually take months. One person can design and build a mobile game on his or her own. Small games can still make big money. The most successful mobile games, such as Candy Crush, earn more than $1 million per day. Each designer hopes his or her game will be the next big hit. Game designers submit about 500 new mobile games to Apple's app store every day.

console—a video game system with controllers and a standalone unit that is plugged into a television

CHAPTER 2
SCRIPT WRITERS

Script writers may have to conduct many hours of research for a single project, which can require hundreds of pages of script.

After a violent storm strands her on a strange island, an adventurer must use her wits and knowledge to survive. She battles wild animals and rugged terrain. She works with hostile locals to eventually escape the island and reunite with her friends. This type of emotional and physical journey is common in video games today, but it was not always that way.

Early game developers designed simple sports and fighting games with little or no scripts. Video games have come a long way since then. Today gamers want powerful stories and intense emotional journeys. The script writer must create these stories. Some writers work at large game studios. Others work as **freelance** writers.

Writers work closely with the game designer. They create scripts based on ideas from the designer. Writers provide scenes, **dialogue**, and **narrative**. They also do research. Writers might research types of vehicles for a car racing game. For a game that takes place in World War II, a writer might study the battles, vehicles, and weapons that were part of the war.

Throughout game production, writers must revise and edit scripts as needed. They adjust story lines and dialogue based on changes that come up during production.

EDUCATION

Script writers should have a strong background in the following STEAM subjects:

- **creative writing**
- **literature**

freelance—paid for each job instead of by the hour or through a yearly salary

dialogue—the words spoken between two or more characters

narrative—the telling of a story

CHAPTER 3

VIDEO GAME PROGRAMMERS

01001000 01001001. What may look like gibberish may actually be important information, written in **binary**. Everything in a video game, including scenes and characters, can be reduced to this simple code. A video game programmer turns scripts, characters, audio, and other elements of a video game into binary code.

Modern video games require millions of lines of code.

Video game programmers usually work for game studios. They complete a variety of tasks to create a video game. A programmer starts work on a new game by reviewing the GDD. He or she then sets to work writing code to create the different elements in the game. Games take a few months to a few years to program.

Next, the programmer creates a **prototype** of the game and shares it with the rest of the team. Based on the prototype, the team offers notes to improve the game. After the prototype is approved, the programmer starts building the full version.

After a game is built, it goes through a quality control process. In this stage, game testers find errors and bugs. The programmers then fix the bugs. The quality control process continues until the game is ready for release.

EDUCATION

Game programmers should have a strong background in the following STEAM subjects:

- **computer science**
- **software engineering**
- **computer programming**
- **calculus**

binary—a system of representing information, used primarily for computers, using only the numbers 0 and 1

prototype—the first trial model of something, made to test and improve the design

CHAPTER 4

3-D MODELERS

All types of imaginary
characters, including dragons,
take shape through 3-D.

SHAPING UP

The computer screen is blank. Suddenly, 3-D
shapes appear: a cylinder, a pyramid, a cube. The shapes
twist, stretch, and bend. As they change, they become less like
simple shapes and more lifelike. Before long, the shapes change
into the detailed image of an enormous, winged dragon. This
transformation is the work of a 3-D modeler.

3-D modelers use computer programs to digitally "sculpt" characters or objects using 3-D **animation**. 3-D modelers do their work using special modeling software. First, 3-D workers build a digital model of the character. They start with basic 3-D shapes. Cubes, cones, and cylinders can all be used. Then they mold the shapes just like an artist working with clay.

A 3-D modeler also digitally adds small details. Should the character have brown eyes or green? How about scars or tattoos? A 3-D modeler can add texture in this stage too. Is the character's skin smooth and glossy? Or is it rough and wrinkly? These small details enhance the character's look, making it realistic.

EDUCATION

3-D modelers should have a strong background in the following STEAM subjects:

- **computer science**
- **animation**
- **body science**

animation—videos made by quickly presenting drawings, one after another, so that the characters seem to be moving

UNDER THE SKIN

3-D modelers must have a good understanding of human **anatomy**. They design characters that look and move in a realistic way. 3-D modelers create the outside, visible parts of the characters. But they also form a skeleton inside. When a skeleton is put in a 3-D model, it is called rigging. The skeleton has joints and a structure like a human body. The skeleton matches up with the 3-D model. The joints determine how the character moves. Some joints twist. Other joints bend. Others do both. The rigging sets the rules for a character's movement.

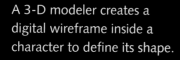

A 3-D modeler creates a digital wireframe inside a character to define its shape.

The cost of making a single modern video game character from start to finish can be up to $80,000.

The modeler also must consider the **medium**. 3-D modeling for a video game is different than for a movie. Traditional film can show limitless details. In a video game, it is important to keep models simple. The game has to process in-game characters in real time every time the player moves. A model that is too complex might crash the game.

ANIMATORS

The 3-D designer passes the model to a team of animators when it is completed. The animators program the movement of the model using computer code. The code tells the models when and how to move. The animators make sure that the movement looks real. Game animation takes a long time. Animators usually complete 5 to 10 seconds of animation per day.

anatomy—the study of the human body

medium—something that communicates messages; TV, movies, and the Internet are all mediums

CHAPTER 5

GRAPHIC DESIGNERS

About 80 percent of graphic designers work for companies. The rest are self-employed and work from home.

Movie posters are often a fan's first glimpse inside a new film. But what should a movie poster show? Should it show characters from the movie or highlight the movie's central idea or theme? The person who makes these artistic decisions is the graphic designer.

Graphic designers create visual art for digital and print publications. They create logos, illustrations, and other graphics. Their work is often used for marketing and advertising.

A graphic designer often works for customers, or clients. Together, they agree on the scope and vision of the project. Graphic designers must think creatively. They brainstorm designs. Designers often draw early concepts by hand. They then use computer software to create final designs. They must be able to balance different elements. Graphic designers create effective designs using color, layout, and text. They also might take data and transform it into easy-to-read charts and diagrams.

Graphic designers often work closely with others. They may partner with writers, illustrators, and photographers to develop creative pieces. When complete, the designer and team present their work. They get feedback from their clients. The designer then makes changes as needed.

EDUCATION

Graphic designers should have a strong background in the following STEAM subjects:

- **fine art**
- **design**
- **marketing**

STEAM FACT

Graphic design may have begun as early as 2700 BC. Ancient Egyptians designed personalized logos for branding farm animals.

CHAPTER 6

MOTION CAPTURE ARTISTS

Professional baseball players are often hired to perform motion capture for their own characters in baseball video games. They swing, catch, and throw while cameras record their movement.

"Lights. Camera. Action!" On the camera's monitor, an enormous wolf growls at the main character. Away from the monitor, a similar scene takes place, with one key difference. Instead of a wolf, there is a person in a skintight suit, covered in what looks like a bunch of Ping-Pong balls. The bizarrely dressed person snarls and takes another step forward. How does the person in the suit become a hungry wolf?

Motion capture (mocap) allows an actor to step into the digital "skin" of a computer-animated character and perform as that character. Mocap artists manage this process.

First, mocap artists help create a rough digital model. Then they fit actors with mocap suits that have markers all over them. As the actors move, special cameras track the markers. While filming, mocap artists use a special monitor. These monitors replace actors with the character models. This lets the director see the digital characters interact with the real-life actors.

After filming, mocap artists fine-tune the scene. They use the actor's performance as their guide. Then the mocap artists add details, such as hair or horns. These details make a character more lifelike. The end result is a realistic digital character.

STEAM FACT

For the 2011 movie *Rise of the Planet of the Apes*, mocap actor Andy Serkis wore 132 markers on his face. These captured facial expressions for his character, an ape named Caesar.

EDUCATION

Motion capture artists should have a strong background in the following STEAM subjects:

- **computer animation**
- **film production**
- **computer science**

CHAPTER 7

VIRTUAL REALITY GAME DEVELOPERS

One gamer may want to experience what it is like to fly above the clouds like an eagle. Another gamer may want to fight zombies to survive. Whatever the interest, VR technology provides endless possibilities for adventure. VR game developers are leading the charge.

As virtual reality becomes more popular, the VR industry is expected to be worth about $140 billion by 2020.

VR game developers guide the production of VR games. VR games immerse the player in imaginary worlds. They do this with special equipment. Goggles and motion-detecting controllers are the most common.

VR developers have a tough job. They must bring together many elements in a VR game. VR games need to have great graphics, and they need to operate smoothly. Glitches or slow graphics can cause motion sickness for a player.

VR developers are looking to the future by creating and testing new technology. Today players can see and hear in a VR environment. VR developers want gamers to be able to feel objects too. Companies that make special clothing outfitted with electronics are turning this into a reality.

EDUCATION

Virtual reality game developers should have a strong background in the following STEAM subjects:

- **visual art**
- **animation**
- **computer science**

CHAPTER 8
AUDIO ENGINEERS

Have you ever tried playing a video game on mute? Does it change your experience? What do you lose when you no longer hear the footsteps of your on-screen character as it runs? When an arrow slams into a tree without a *thunk* sound, is it as scary? Video games depend on sound to make them fun and engaging. Audio engineers are the people who record and **mix** sound for video games.

Audio engineers are highly skilled in mixing sounds. They might work with hundreds of thousands of different sounds and lines of dialogue for a single video game.

Technology plays a big role in audio production. Audio engineers first set up microphones. The microphones record dialogue and sound effects. The microphones connect to digital-audio **interfaces**. These turn the sound into a digital format that a computer can process. Once it is on the computer, the engineer mixes the audio.

Audio engineers need an artistic ear. Audio engineers usually mix on a digital audio workstation (DAW), a computer program designed to mix audio. Their work on a DAW system includes adding in other elements. Wind or water sound effects can enhance an environment. The engineer layers on filters to change how audio sounds. DAWs typically have thousands of filters. One filter makes voices sound clearer. Another makes voices sound as if they are coming through a telephone.

EDUCATION

Audio engineers should have a strong background in the following STEAM subjects:

- **audio production**
- **communications**

mix—to digitally combine, edit, and add effects to sounds that come from more than one source

interface—equipment used to connect and communicate between different computer systems

CHAPTER 9
TOY DESIGNERS

Two cars race along a track. They are neck and neck. Approaching the jump, both drivers give their cars maximum power. The cars fly off the track and seem to float for just a second. Then they come crashing down. One car made the jump and continues along. The second car tumbles to the carpet, landing upside-down with wheels spinning. Race car tracks are fun and exciting toys, but who designs them?

A toy designer invents new toys. These designers are also called toy makers, toy engineers, or toy inventors. Toy designers can create products in many different toy categories. These include dolls, action figures, toy vehicles, and games.

STEAM FACT

Barbie dolls are one of the best-selling toys of all time. Customers around the world have bought 1 billion dolls.

Mattel cofounder Ruth Handler created Barbie in 1959. She named the doll after her daughter, Barbara.

A toy designer must follow many steps when creating a new toy. First, a toy designer develops a concept. The designer might start with hand-drawn sketches. They then work with computer programs to create a digital version. A prototype is built once a toy idea is designed and approved.

Toy designers often test their toy prototypes with kids to see if they like them. The designer considers making improvements based on the results. Once perfected, a toy finally enters production.

EDUCATION

Toy designers should have a strong background in the following STEAM subjects:

- **visual art**
- **child behavior and early learning**
- **engineering**

CHAPTER 10
USER RESEARCHERS

User researchers work with gamers to test new video game consoles.

Successful video games make serious money. That is why companies want to make sure their products work well. Game studios turn to user researchers for help. User researchers are professional **psychologists**. They study people who play video games. Then they use the study results to help companies develop better games. User researchers might work for game studios or run their own business. Some researchers even make their own games.

Most user researchers work with a video game's production team to discuss goals for player experience. User researchers design studies to see if these goals are reached.

Researchers then bring in players from the **target audience**. The researchers use video cameras and one-way mirrors to watch people while they play games. A user researcher also gives surveys to players to learn more about their habits and opinions.

After running the tests, the researcher organizes the data. Then the user researcher studies the results. They use **statistics** to draw conclusions.

EDUCATION

User researchers should have a strong background in the following STEAM subjects:

- **psychology**
- **market research**
- **statistics**

psychologist—a person who studies people's minds, emotions, and the ways they behave

target audience—the group of people that a particular product, such as a movie, book, or video game, is intended for

statistics—the study of numerical data

GLOSSARY

anatomy (uh-NA-tuh-mee)—the study of the human body

animation (a-nuh-MAY-shuhn)—videos made by quickly presenting drawings, one after another, so that the characters seem to be moving

binary (BI-nuh-ree)—a system of representing information, used primarily for computers, using only the numbers 0 and 1

concept (KAHN-sept)—an idea for a new way to build or create something

console (KAHN-sohl)—a video game system with controllers and a standalone unit that is plugged into a television

dialogue (DYE-uh-lawg)—the words spoken between two or more characters

freelance (FREE-lants)—paid for each job instead of by the hour or through a yearly salary

interface (IN-ter-fays)—equipment used to connect and communicate between different computer systems

medium (MEE-dee-um)—something that communicates messages; TV, movies, and the Internet are all mediums

mix (MIKS)—to digitally combine, edit, and add effects to sounds that come from more than one source

narrative (NA-ruh-tiv)—the telling of a story

prototype (PROH-tuh-tipe)—the first trial model of something, made to test and improve the design

psychologist (sye-KOH-luh-jist)—a person who studies people's minds, emotions, and the ways they behave

statistics (stuh-TISS-tiks)—the study of numerical data

STEAM (STEEM)—the abbreviation for science, technology, engineering, art, and mathematics

target audience (TAHR-git AW-dee-unts)—the group of people that a particular product, such as a movie, book, or video game, is intended for

READ MORE

Ceceri, Kathy. *Video Games: Design and Code Your Own Adventure with 17 Projects.* Build It Yourself. White River Junction, Vt.: Nomad Press, 2015.

Cornell, Kari. *Minecraft Creator Markus "Notch" Persson.* STEM Trailblazer Bios. Minneapolis: Lerner Publications, 2016.

Edelman, Brad. *Computer Programming: Learn It, Try It!* Science Brain Builders. North Mankato, Minn.: Capstone, 2018.

INTERNET SITES

Use FactHound to find Internet sites related to this book.

Visit *www.facthound.com*

Just type in 9781543530933 and go.

Check out projects, games and lots more at
www.capstonekids.com

INDEX